OCEAN ANIMAL GROUPS

by

Rebecca Phillips-Bartlett

BEARPORT
PUBLISHING

Minneapolis, Minnesota

Credits

All images are courtesy of Shutterstock.com, unless otherwise specified. With thanks to Getty Images, Thinkstock Photo, and iStockphoto. Recurring images – Miceking, Ihor Biliavskyi, Kazakov Maksim, Nadzin, Bur_malin, Andrii_Malysh, Zaie, Alexander A. Nedviga. Cover – Laura Dts, Nadzin, akingsley, Thierry Eidenweil, Zaie, PictuLandra. 2–3 – Willyam Bradberry. 4–5 – Maya Parfentieva, Rich Carey, Andrii_Malysh, Manuel Balesteri. 6–7 – Jag_cz, Viacheslav Lopatin. 8–9 – Goinyk Production, Thierry Eidenweil, Niklas Prescher. 10–11 – Yann hubert, Tomas Kotouc, KittyVector, Alex Rush, Lewis Burnett. 12–13 – Rich Carey, V_E. 14–15 – Willyam Bradberry, Andrea Izzotti, DianaFinch. 16–17 – fred goldstein, worldswildlifewonders, Chase Dekker, MansonFotos, burbura. 18–19 – Tory Kallman, slowmotiongli, Alfmaler. 20–21 – Dotted Yeti, Alfmaler. 22–23 – Vlad61, akingsley.

Bearport Publishing Company Product Development Team

President: Jen Jenson; Director of Product Development: Spencer Brinker; Managing Editor: Allison Juda; Associate Editor: Naomi Reich; Associate Editor: Tiana Tran; Senior Designer: Colin O'Dea; Associate Designer: Elena Klinkner; Associate Designer: Kayla Eggert; Product Development Assistant: Owen Hamlin

Library of Congress Cataloging-in-Publication Data

Names: Phillips-Bartlett, Rebecca, 1999- author.
Title: Ocean animal groups / Rebecca Phillips-Bartlett.
Description: Minneapolis, Minnesota : Bearport Publishing Company, [2024] |
   Series: Wild animal families | Includes index.
Identifiers: LCCN 2023029638 (print) | LCCN 2023029639 (ebook) | ISBN
   9798889163206 (library binding) | ISBN 9798889163251 (paperback) | ISBN
   9798889163299 (ebook)
Subjects: LCSH: Marine animals--Juvenile literature.
Classification: LCC QL122.2 .P495 2024 (print) | LCC QL122.2 (ebook) |
   DDC 591.77--dc23/eng/20230713
LC record available at https://lccn.loc.gov/2023029638
LC ebook record available at https://lccn.loc.gov/2023029639

For more information, write to Bearport Publishing, 5357 Penn Avenue South, Minneapolis, MN 55419.

CONTENTS

WILD ANIMAL FAMILIES

Earth is full of amazing animals. Many of them live in groups. This helps animals stay safe. It also makes it easier for them to find food and a place to stay.

Many different animal families make their homes in oceans.

Let's visit different animal families in their watery **habitats**. The oceans have everything the plants and animals there need to live.

IN THE OCEAN

Oceans cover most of Earth. In fact, there is way more water than land on our planet. All this salty water is filled with many different habitats.

There are five oceans in the world. These are the Arctic, Atlantic, Indian, Pacific, and Southern Oceans.

Arctic Ocean

Atlantic Ocean

Pacific Ocean

Indian Ocean

Southern Ocean

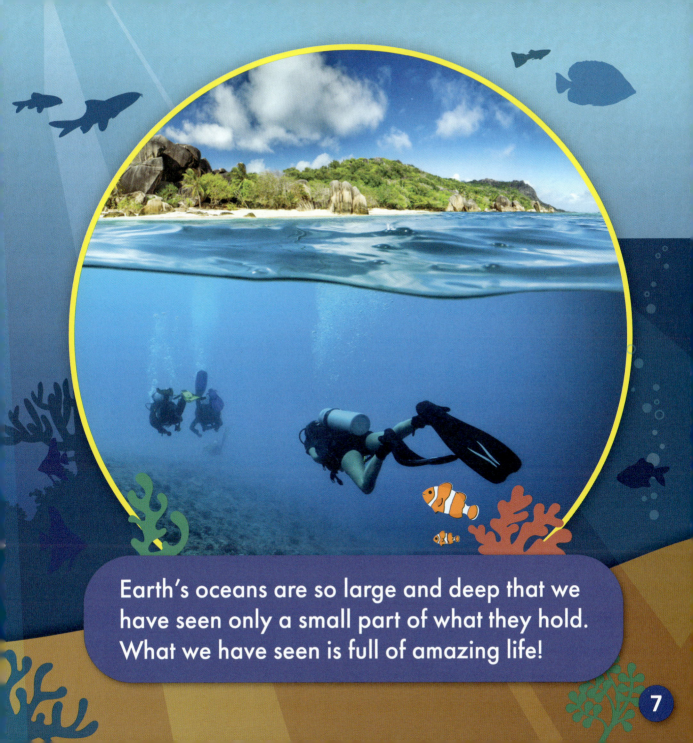

Earth's oceans are so large and deep that we have seen only a small part of what they hold. What we have seen is full of amazing life!

CORAL POLYPS

Polyps are tiny creatures that live in large groups called colonies. They build hard shells called corals. Groups of polyps make coral reefs.

Polyps in the reef work together to get food. They also play an important role for others in the habitat. Coral reefs are home to thousands of other animals.

Polyps use their tentacles to get food from the water around them.

Polyp tentacles

SHARKS

There are more than 500 kinds of sharks. Some live alone. Others get together to hunt or travel in groups.

A group of sharks can be called a shiver, frenzy, or herd.

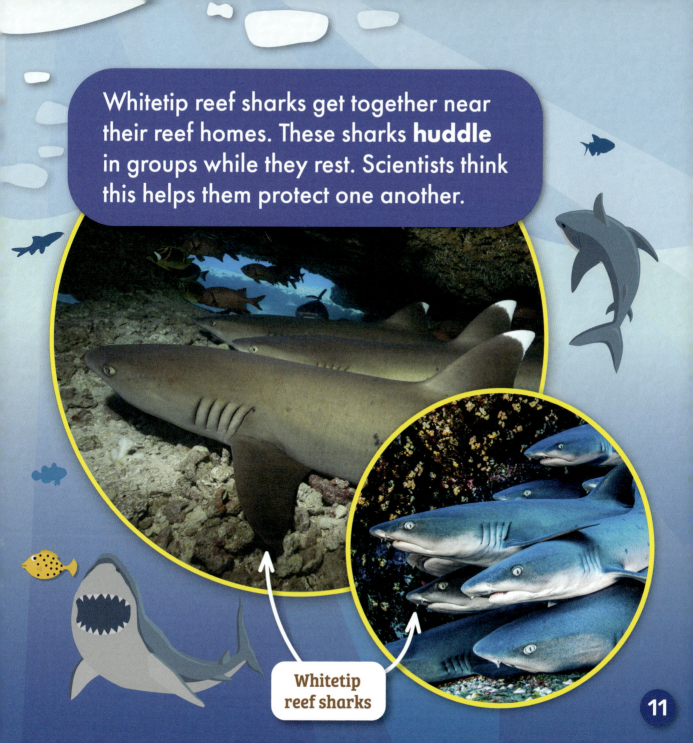

Whitetip reef sharks get together near their reef homes. These sharks **huddle** in groups while they rest. Scientists think this helps them protect one another.

Whitetip reef sharks

FISH

There are about 34,000 kinds of fish in the oceans. They live in differently sized groups. Different kinds of fishy groups are called different things.

There have been fish on Earth for more than 500 million years.

A large gathering of fish that swims together in a loose group is called a shoal (SHOLE). Many fish of the same **species** that swim as one is called a school.

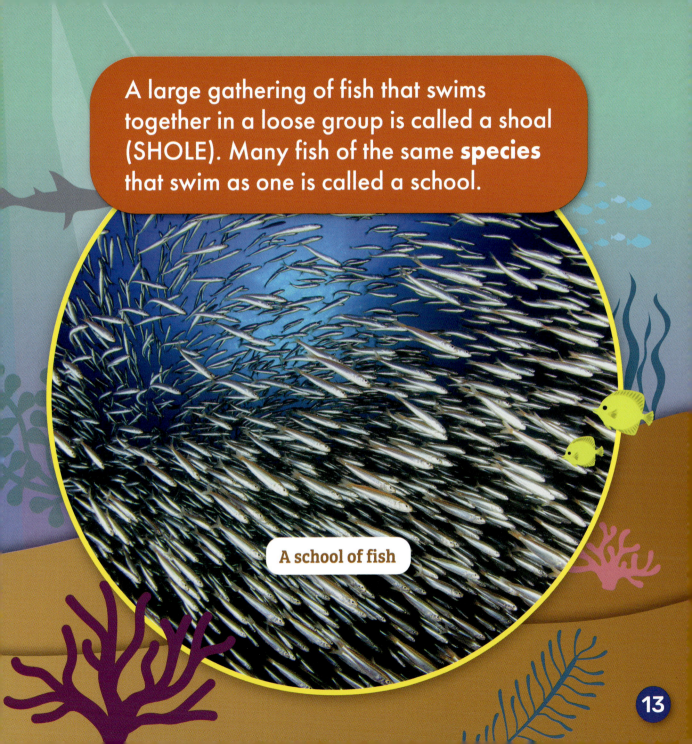

A school of fish

DOLPHINS

Dolphins live in groups called pods. They work together to hunt **prey**, stay away from **predators**, and take care of one another. Pods get bigger and smaller as dolphins join and leave these groups.

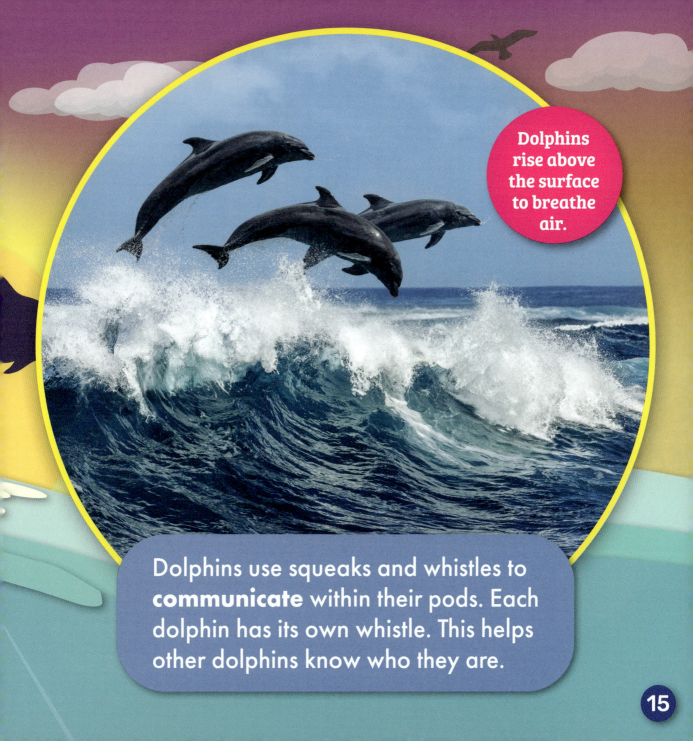

Dolphins rise above the surface to breathe air.

Dolphins use squeaks and whistles to **communicate** within their pods. Each dolphin has its own whistle. This helps other dolphins know who they are.

SEA OTTERS

Sea otters spend most of their lives in the ocean. They bob along in the water in small groups.

Sea otters have a special way of staying together when they are sleeping. They hold hands and float together in the water. This keeps them from drifting apart.

A raft

Groups of sea otters resting together are called rafts.

17

ORCAS

Orcas also live in family pods. Unlike the changing pods of dolphins, orca pods stay the same. Each one has its own **culture**.

Orcas live in pods with about 5 to 30 animals.

A pod's culture is passed down within the group. This includes the kind of food a pod eats and the noises the orcas make.

NARWHALS

Narwhals live in ocean groups called pods or blessings. Usually, there are about 10 to 20 narwhals in each. But sometimes, there can be more than a hundred when they are **migrating**.

Narwhals are known for their single tusks. Some people think the animals use their tusks to **sense** things around them.

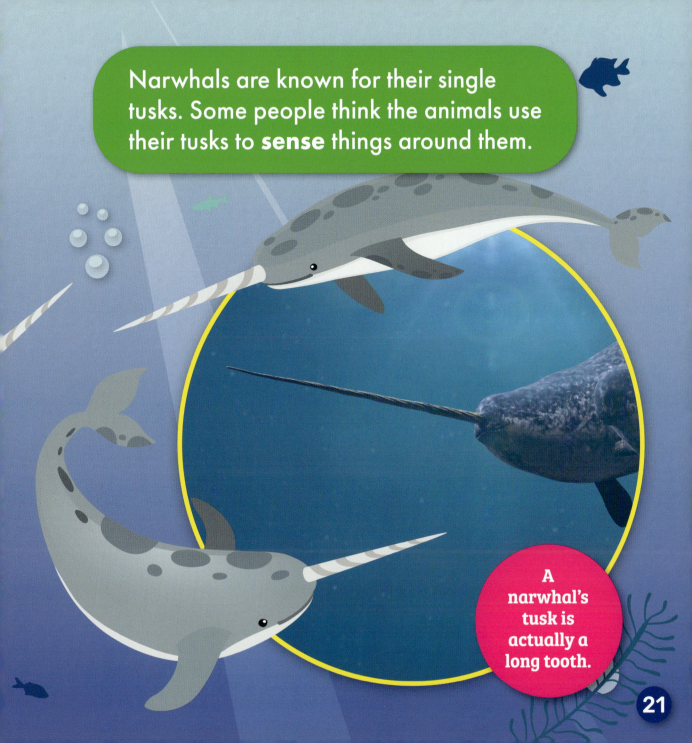

A narwhal's tusk is actually a long tooth.

FAMILY FOCUS

Many amazing animal family groups live in the ocean. These groups are all different in a lot of ways. However, they do have some things in common.

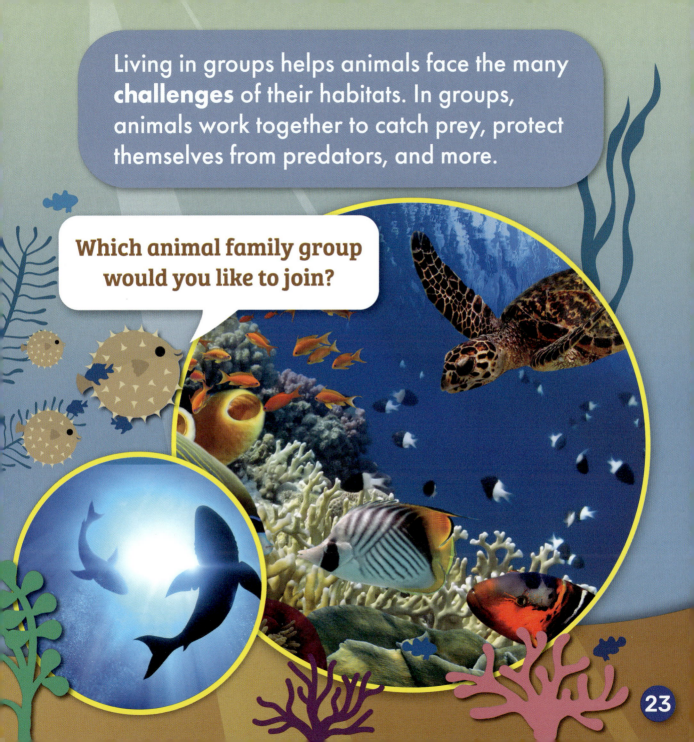

Living in groups helps animals face the many **challenges** of their habitats. In groups, animals work together to catch prey, protect themselves from predators, and more.

Which animal family group would you like to join?

GLOSSARY

challenges problems or tasks that need extra work or effort to do

communicate to pass on ideas, thoughts, or feelings to others

culture the traditions, ideas, and ways of life of a group

habitats places in nature where plants or animals normally live

huddle to gather together in a close group

migrating moving from one area to another

predators animals that hunt other animals for food

prey animals hunted by other animals

sense to feel or detect something

species groups that animals are divided into, according to things they have in common

INDEX